A TRIP TO THE
GROCERY STORE

Josie Keogh

PowerKiDS
press™

New York

Published in 2013 by The Rosen Publishing Group, Inc.
29 East 21st Street, New York, NY 10010

First Edition

Editor: Amelie von Zumbusch
Book Design: Ashley Drago

Photo Credits: Cover, p. 23 Shutterstock.com; p. 5 Peter Dazeley/Riser/Getty Images; pp. 6, 9 Hemera/Thinkstock; p. 11 Ed Lallo/Photolibrary/Getty Images; p. 12 Noel Hendrickson/Digital Vision/Thinkstock; p. 15 Andersen Ross/Iconica/Getty Images; p. 16 Taxi/Getty Images; p. 19 iStockphoto/Thinkstock; p. 20 Photodisc/Thinkstock.

Library of Congress Cataloging-in-Publication Data

Keogh, Josie.
 A trip to the grocery store / by Josie Keogh. — 1st ed.
   p. cm. — (Powerkids readers: my community)
Includes index.
ISBN 978-1-4488-7403-3 (library binding) — ISBN 978-1-4488-7482-8 (pbk.) —
ISBN 978-1-4488-7556-6 (6-pack)
1. Supermarkets—Juvenile literature. 2. Grocery shopping–Juvenile literature. I. Title.
HF5469.K46 2013
381'.456413—dc
                        2011049392

Manufactured in the United States of America

CPSIA Compliance Information: Batch #CS12PK: For Further Information contact Rosen Publishing, New York, New York at 1-800-237-9932

CONTENTS

The grocery store sells food.

There are many kids there.

Jess gets food for lunch.

Dan picks out fruit.

RED DELICIOUS
$1.19 LB

11

Kat finds milk!

Jack gets meat for dinner.

The label says what is in a food.

17

Mike likes rye bread.

You pay right before you leave.

Jane carries a big bag home.

WORDS TO KNOW

cashier:
A person people
give money to.

dairy: Having to
do with milk.

deli counter:
A place that sells
cold meats.

INDEX

WEBSITES

Due to the changing nature of
Internet links, PowerKids Press has
developed an online list of websites
related to the subject of this book.
This site is updated regularly. Please
use this link to access the list:
www.powerkidslinks.com/pkrc/groc/